A LECTURE ON LECTURES

HOGARTH LECTURES ON LITERATURE

Editors: GEORGE RYLANDS, LEONARD WOOLF

A LECTURE ON
LECTURES

Introductory Volume

By
SIR ARTHUR QUILLER-COUCH (" Q ")

THE HOGARTH PRESS

40-42 WILLIAM IV STREET,
LONDON, W.C.2

Published by
The Hogarth Press Ltd
London

★

Clarke, Irwin & Company Ltd
Toronto

First published 1927
Second impression 1950

PRINTED BY THE REPLIKA PROCESS
IN GREAT BRITAIN BY
LUND HUMPHRIES
LONDON · BRADFORD

A LECTURE ON LECTURES

Talking of education, " People have nowadays (said he) got a
strange opinion that everything should be taught by
Lectures. Now, I cannot see that Lectures can do so much
good as reading the Books from which the Lectures are taken.
I know nothing that can be best taught by Lectures except
where experiments are to be shown. You may teach
Chemistry by Lectures. You cannot teach making of
shoes by Lectures ! "—BOSWELL, *Life of Dr Johnson*
(*ætat.* 57).

We talked of the difference between the mode of education at
Oxford and that in those Colleges where instruction is
chiefly conveyed by Lectures. *Johnson*: " Lectures were
once useful ; but now, when all can read, and Books are
so numerous, Lectures are unnecessary. If your attention fails, and you miss a part of the Lecture, it is lost.
You cannot go back as you can upon a Book." Dr Scott
agreed with him. " But yet (said I), Doctor Scott, you
yourself gave Lectures at Oxford." He smiled. " You
laughed (then said I) at those who came to you."—*Ibid.*
(Johnson, *ætat.* 72).

I

To the first of the above passages Mr Augustine
Birrell, in his sprightly edition of the *Life*, appends
a footnote—"Lecturers are very fond of this

quotation—but they go on lecturing all the same."

I propose that we examine Dr Johnson's *dicta* upon lecturing, and maybe our investigations will even elicit the secret of Dr Scott's smile. He lived to become Lord Stowell and was reasonably addicted to the bottle: but the secret lies deeper than *that*. As for Boswell's remark—well, it is Boswell purely reported by himself—and, of course, killed the conversation which he strove officiously to keep alive.

On the face of it this looks like Johnson's habitual common-sense—and so it is, up to a point, as we shall see. Yet we may remind ourselves that he survives for us, as the massive man he was, rather by virtue of his reported talk and dialectic than through his books. Socrates, too, loved a book. Finding his friend Phædius with one hidden under his cloak, he proposes that they walk out and read it by the shaded Ilyssus. "For," says he, "city-man tho' I am, you have found a spell with which to draw me out into the country, like a hungry cow when a bough or a bunch of fruit is waved before her nose. For only hold up a book before, and in like manner you may entice me all round Attica, nay, round the wide world." Yet Socrates who loved a book never wrote one, so far as we know; and his gigantic fame rests wholly on descriptions and his talk reported by faithful disciples, as does that of a greater than Socrates on accounts and reported sayings in the Gospels.

Johnson himself confessed to having "cut" lectures at Pembroke College, Oxford, yet not without a tinge of remorse. "Indeed," said he, "I did not attend him (his tutor, Mr Jordan) much.

"The first day after I came to College I waited upon him and then stayed away four. On the sixth, Mr Jordan asked me why I had not attended. I answered that I had been sliding in Christ Church meadow. . . "

"That, Sir," suggested Boswell, "was great fortitude of mind."

Johnson. "No, Sir, stark insensibility."

II

But before attempting any defence of lecturing I wish to summon up a deal of the devil's advocacy against it, and even to append my own. In the *New Review* of May 1890 that gentle, wise and possibly misguided man, Henry Sidgwick, who planted and watered Women's Colleges in

Cambridge, published a most wise "Lecture against Lecturing." For so gentle a man (but one learns to suspect the serpent beneath so obvious a dove) he put it boldly:

> I regard the ordinary expository lecture—in most subjects, and so far as the most intelligent class of students are concerned—as an antiquated survival; a relic of the times before the printing-press was invented; maintained partly by the mere conservatism of habit and the prestige of ancient tradition, partly by the difficulty—which I quite admit—of finding a right substitute for it.

(I shall discuss this difficulty by and by.) Sidgwick admits that he is pleading mainly on behalf of what he calls "the élite of academic students" —or, as I should now prefer to call them in an English University, "undergraduates," leaving you to interpret my preference for that old name as you will. He defines these as "the intelligent and industrious youth who have been trained from childhood to the habit of deriving ideas from books, and are able and willing to apply prolonged labour and concentrated attention to the methodical perusal of books under the direction of their teachers." He implies further that his remarks must considerably narrow his ground, when he adds that they have no reference to that large part of the community "that has never acquired a thorough mastery of the art of reading books. Nor," he goes on, still narrowing his point of attack, "do they refer to the class of so-called academic students [1] who require the discipline of schoolboys. It may be necessary," he continues, "to drive these latter into lecture-rooms in order to increase the chance of their obtaining the required instruction somehow."

I say "increase the chance," because it is by no means certain that young people of this turn of mind will actually drink of the fountain of knowledge, even if they are led to it daily between 10 a.m. and 1 p.m. But the compulsion may, no doubt, increase the chance of their imbibing knowledge, since it is difficult to find amusement during a lecture which will distract one's attention completely from the lecturer, although I have known instances in which the difficulty has been successfully overcome by patient ingenuity.

III

Now I am, for sundry reasons, one of the last men likely to resent the invention of the printing-press; and, to prove the good faith of this asser-

---

[1] So-called " academic students " ? But who, save a so-called " educationist " ever in England called them so ?

tion here and now, will present the plaintiff's advocate with a few admissions—nay, arguments —for his case of Books *versus* Lectures as engines of mental instruction.

To begin with, the voice of the lecturer, whether audible or not, must run on and on for his allotted hour or (if he be wise) his fifty minutes. All that time he must be filing out his words one by one, and slowly by preference, through what a Greek would have called "the narrow gateway of his lips," for each one of his audience to re-form and regiment these units, so to speak, according to the unseen will behind the gate—a continuous process on both sides; and because the speaker has prepared and arranged his argument, his discourse should be allowed to run its appointed length by the clock, and uninterrupted, to the conclusion or conclusions towards which he is making.

I assume, of course, that the lecturer *has* marshalled his argument so that it lacks not (as the old divine puts it in Thomas Love Peacock) the primary requisites of a head and a tail. And I am thinking for the moment—and for the moment only—of public, or "set" lectures, at which the good manners of our English Universities forbid audible interruptions. Nay, at such lectures even the silent taking of notes—a mannerly practice, since it politely implies that the thing said deserves recording—is a distraction for the listener, who, even though skilled in shorthand, will be apt, in the hurry of doing two things at one time, to hear the beginning of the next sentence inattentively and so let slip, maybe, the nexus of the argument or miss an essential point.

In "class" lectures—and especially in such as deal with the interpretation of texts and minute points—some play of question and answer should be permitted and even sparingly encouraged; while in discussion classes (or *symposia* or *seminars*, as you choose to call them) dialectic is the essence of the game. But concerning public lectures, let us agree with Plutarch that "a youth is at all times sure to find silence a credit to him, but especially here." A serious objection still lies against such lectures. If a student take notes, his ear is distracted; if he do not, his memory may let slip some cardinal point.[1]

[1] I have observed judges in Courts of Assize to miss an immediate, small, but possibly vital point of evidence while

IV

Now at both of these points the printed book has obvious advantages over the spoken lecture, and indeed apparently does away with the dilemma. The reader of a book can take it at his own *tempo*, not hurried by the lecturer's pace. He can bend his mind to it at his own convenience, not catching up his gown to attend on a time-table, not pushing for a seat if he be late and the seats crowded. If he find a difficulty here and there, he can pause at any point, turn back, re-read. No continuous strain of attention is required; for, while the spoken lecture may induce somnolence and the printed page a somnolence even deeper, yet with the advantages of privacy, you can lay the book at any point face downward on your knee, turn back on awaking, and recapture your interest. You cannot do this with a lecturer—who, moreover, has possibly by this time gone home.

For one further natural advantage of the book over the lecture, our experience has, I suggest, taught most of us that memorising depends a

absorbed in catching up with their own longhand notes. Surely in these days of accurate stenography a judge should be released to concentrate his whole attention on the hearing.

great deal on *visualising*—that when we wish, for example, to hunt back a quotation in a book, we have a mental photograph of the page on which it occurred, and its place and setting on that page. We have no such adventitious aid when we memorise by the ear alone.

You will agree perhaps that by this time the devil's advocate has been given a fair, if not a complete hearing. If so, let me put up some **few** pleas for the defence. And I shall lay little stress on the plea of history, that the way of lecturing has been the way of our Universities since their foundation. One might, indeed, wax enthusiastic over what little is known of the great line of European lecturers, each a charmer of souls in his day, choosing such names as Parmenides, Aristotle, Plotinus, Epictetus, Abelard, Aquinas, Roger Bacon, Wyclif, Erasmus, and Colet and Grocyn—famous men and (slightly to adapt the Son of Siraeh)—

> Leaders of the people by their knowledge of learning meet for the people, wise and eloquent in their instructions. Such as found out musical tunes, and recited verses in writing. [Moderately] rich men, furnished with ability, living [so far as religious or democratic spite allowed them] peaceably in their habitations.

Yes, and to speak particularly of those medieval times—of those "Dark Ages" over which it is the fashion just now to spread so much colour-wash—one might draw most moving pictures of high-roads dotted with wandering scholars, of lads with knapsacks by garden gates in remotest villages, waving farewell to their families because, over the mountains or up from the coast, report has come that somewhere—in Paris or Bologna, or Leyden or Oxford or Cambridge—someone is saying things youth craves to hear, and saying them "not as the scribes," but freshly yet with authority.   I have quoted on another occasion my favourite story of three scholars of Oxford, so poor that they possessed but one "cappa" and gown amongst them.   They took it in turns therefore, and when one went to lecture the other two kept to their lodging.   The three lived habitually on bread with soup and a little wine, tasting meat only on Sundays and feasts of the Church.   Yet one of them, Richard of Chichester, who lived to earn consecration as a Saint—*Sæpe retulit quod nunquam in vita sua tam jucundam tam delectabilem duxerat vitam*—would often recall that never had he lived so jollily, so delectably.

Yes, but printed books in those days were

none, and manuscripts so costly that the poor scholar had to rely on what chance he was given to copy them or on his own lecture notes. Thus the Clerk in Chaucer, who learnt by charitable support of his friends,

> was lever have at his beddes heed
> Twenty bokes clad in blak or reed
> Of Aristotle and his philosophye
> Than robes riche or fithele or gay sautrye,

whereas, nowadays, most of the necessary books are cheap. The rarer texts, if he be a graduate here in Cambridge, he can borrow from our University here: if an undergraduate, consult in it. Free public libraries are accessible in all our great cities, in almost every township, and of late—thanks to the liberal policy of the Carnegie Trustees—rural libraries are being disseminated by our Local Education Authorities, on rail and lorry, to the remotest villages where books are asked for—even expensive books and books of higher learning. So we come back to the questions: Are lectures really necessary any longer? Are they not for the most part a superstition? And, anyhow, have we not too many of them?

V

Well, while lectures continue to be given and (which is far more important) men and women continue to attend them, it were unwise, I think, to reprobate a human function or a form of public enjoyment which, for reasons however obscure, apparently ministers, without bloodshed or cruelty, to some natural instinct. I have been talking hitherto (let me remind you) chiefly of public lectures—of *conférences* as the French call them. And concerning these I admit at once that the instinct of many to instruct from a platform "the more cultivated portion of the ignorant"—as Stevenson puts it—is ruthless and indomitable. Those of you who enjoy that little masterpiece of levity, *The Wrong Box* (and I would they were all of you), will remember how the passion seized and grew upon Mr Joseph Finsbury to the detriment of his leather business.

A taste for general information, not promptly checked, had soon begun to sap his manhood. There is no passion more debilitating to the mind, unless perhaps it be that itch of public speaking which it not infrequently accompanies or begets. The two were conjoined in the case of Joseph; the acute stage of this double malady, that in which the patient delivers gratuitous lectures, soon declared itself with severity, and not many years had passed over his head before he would have travelled thirty miles to address an infant school.

Now if there be anything that irritates me in public or daily social life—possibly as a burnt child exposed by fate to many fires—it is that air of academic superiority commonly, but erroneously, labelled "the Oxford manner." (There is more than enough of it infesting Cambridge.) And if offensive when a member of one University uses or suggests it towards the inhabitants of another, I find it doubly offensive when a member of either uses it towards the rest of the world. We know that we are fortunate, and should silently thank God for it: also we have learned, up here, to appraise the various values of a "University education"—how much it *can*, how little and even worse, it *may* mean. So, when I say of extramural popular lectures that, in my opinion, the chief fault with them is their multitude—that there are too many of them— you must in the first place, if you will, discount the feelings of one who spends some part of his time in declining the honour of giving them; and, further, accept my word that of the work

done throughout England by the University
Extension movement, by the Gilchrist Lectures,
by the efforts of the Workers' Educational Asso-
ciation—while of this last, deploring the term
"Workers" because it implies a distinction at
once false and invidious.

All Balzac's novels occupy one shelf,

and Balzac was not a "worker"—or was he?—
accept my word (I say) that of the work done by
these and other societies the benefit to many has
been priceless.   Also, one does not forget Emerson
and the use to which Emerson turned the popular
lecture.

Still, the fact remains that the numbers of
those who "give their minds" to a public lecture,
and those who attend it as something "given to
their minds" (like a drug), are disappointing in
proportion, and for the devoted ministers of all
these "movements" faith, hope, and charity
continue to be the cardinal virtues.

But so far as one can speak generally of public
lectures, whether given within or without the
University, I should plead the following advantages on which it stands up, and perhaps will always
assert itself, against the competition of books.

1. In the first place the hearer comes to it in a certain state of excitement, which differs from the excitement of opening a book, though it be but the excitement (if the lecturer be known to attract) of finding a good seat. Some amount of the sporting instinct must surely animate the patience of those who wait in long lines at the pit or gallery entrance of a theatre—though our star actors may not allow this. The curtain, so to speak, is advertised to rise at a certain hour. Now, to a book you can come in your own time and with a reasonable certainty of being able to "find the place."

2. Further, this excitement of anticipation is naturally high when the lecturer standing at the desk is a man his audience know to be a man who has fought his fight in life and to be honoured even for his scars. I still recall the thrill, for instance, of listening to Ruskin—cadaverous, his voice attenuated as a ghost's, his reason trembling at the last. But there was the man, and he was speaking; and behind the mask and beneath the neat buttoned frock-coat one divined the noble brain and heart defeated, worshipped the noble wounds.

It is obvious, of course, that this form of excitation admits of any number of degrees.

3. Further again—and you may take it from one whose own performance in an inaugural lecture was criticised by a descriptive reporter as "harsh and immelodious"—there is, with those few who know how to employ it, a penetrating power of persuasion in the human voice which the secondary hieroglyphics of print cannot match; an intimacy, even with large audiences, not to be challenged as yet—improvable as they are—even by the devices of broadcasting. Politicians know this only too well.

4. And—lastly here—I have many times, as a listener, felt the truth underlying that famous prayer of St Chrysostom's, the "Golden-mouthed," even when the voice has been no Chrysostom's but that of a very poor orator indeed. I remember, for example, being aware of it once and almost poignantly while assisting at an address by Lord Goschen, now many years dead, whose subject was not so attractive that I can remember it at this distance of time, and whose voice was wrung with such difficulty from the larynx that, as he tugged with both hands at his shirt-collar, he suggested a painful struggle with strangulation. But there he was; a strong man talking with knowledge and a sort of dark

enthusiasm: and, sentence by sentence, he en-
forced the high contagion.   The truth I mean is
this,—that when a number of persons are met for
a purpose in itself unselfish (and the love of
learning is *that*). there often prevails over the
assembly a strange congregational spirit, recog-
nisably good by any individual member, yet not
his own, yet nothing he consciously brought; but
unlocking, rather, some sense that men have more
good in common than they pretend to, if only
some other man have the gift or art to unlock it.

It is rare, of course, to find these four virtues
that I have named—expectation and reverence
in the audience, sincerity and charm in the lecturer—all conjoined.   But the true test of an art
is its highest possibility.   I invite, then, anyone
to turn to Hazlitt's famous essay of his "First
Acquaintance with Poets," and to read the pages
describing his first audience of Coleridge's preach-
ing; to the page that begins with—

> It was in January of 1728 that I rose one morning
> before daylight to walk ten miles in the mud to hear
> this celebrated person preach,

and ends with the rapturous homeward journey.

> The sun, that was still labouring pale and wan
> through the sky, obscured by thick clouds, seemed an

emblem of the *good cause*; and the cold dark drops
of dew that hung half-melted on the beard of the
thistle, had something genial and refreshing in them;
for there was a spirit of hope and youth in all nature
that turned everything into good.

I invite him (I say) to read Hazlitt's essay,
and if he himself have never returned like Browning's David from such an experience—

I know not too well how I found my way home in
the night.
There were witnesses cohort about me, to left and
to right,
Angels' powers . . .

—and I defy him to say that, at its best, the lecture
can ever be conquered by time or cold print.

VI

But—to descend to a colder topic—the simple
and sufficient answer to those who maintain that
the Book has more or less antiquated the Lecture
and should largely supersede it, is that there are
lectures *and* lectures; the intention, use, subject,
and method of which fall into separate categories:
to confuse these categories in any general pro-
position is, by cross-dividing, to mix up things

that differ, as did the Oxford tradesman who advertised himself as "University, Pork and Family Butcher." In *use*, for example, there are public lectures and "class" lectures, and the intention may be either to stimulate the hearer's interest, to direct his subsequent reading, or again to impart knowledge directly—three very different things, which again may yet be combined in various proportions so long as they are not confused.

Then for *subject*. Your lecture may be on classical literature, philology, archæology; on mathematics; on mental or moral philosophy; on doctrinal or historical theology or some Biblical text; on medicine, anatomy, pathology; on engineering; on astronomy, chemistry, physics, astrophysics; on the literature of your mother-tongue. Obviously this diversity of subject demands great variety of method in the proportion between observation and experiment, in our use of the printed book whether as material or as an instrument. You cannot experiment with the planets or with Boswell's *Life of Johnson* as you can with an engine or with a gas.

Sidgwick, of course, recognises this. He therefore rules out of the ring, (1) "dialectical" lectures —to the meaning of which term I shall presently

come; (2) lectures which he calls "exhibitory"—
that is to say, those in which the lecturer makes
an exhibition, not necessarily of himself, but of
experiments or specimens—gas (shall we say),
fossils, that sort of thing.   (3) He ends by ruling
out, with the comprehensive gesture of a true
philosopher, lectures on art or literature—
and lectures "on any subject whatever that are
intended to stimulate interest rather than to
convey information."   "For these purposes," he
adds, "I conceive that the use of lectures will
increase rather than diminish as civilisation pro-
gresses"—a distant prospect! but tinged with
characteristic benevolence.

Having thus cleared the ring of all but the
"expository lecture" (as he calls it), "the ordinary
expository lecture in which the lecturer's function
is merely to impart instruction by reading or
saying a series of words that might be written or
printed"—a definition on which our pugilist,
having armed himself with three question-begging
words and a trope, gets going at last on the
"expository" lecture—he draws us (but surely
he needed not to stray so far afield for it) his
first experience at a lecture by an eminent pro-
fessor in a German University.

I went at the hour announced; the small lecture-room gradually filled, becoming even fuller than was quite agreeable in the heats of July; and I waited in expectant curiosity. The eminent man came in, according to custom, punctually at the quarter; he carried in his hand a manuscript yellow with age: he did not seem to look at his audience, but fixing his eyes on the manuscript he began to read it aloud with slow monotonous utterance. I glanced around the room: every pupil that I could see was bending over his notebook, writing as hard as he could. The unfamiliar surroundings and the unfamiliar language stimulated my imagination, and I fancied myself back in a world more than four centuries older, in which it had not yet occurred to Coster or Gutenberg that it would be a convenience to use movable types for the multiplication of copies of MS. I have since listened to many other lectures in German University lecture-rooms, some of which have been admirably delivered: still, the effect of this first experience has not been entirely effaced.

VII

Well, now, let us deal for a minute or two historically with this "expository" lecture which Sidgwick—partly excused by the fashion of his time—chose to criticise from so Teutonic an angle.

I suppose that the lectures so penibly attended

by Richard of Chichester and his poor fellow-scholars of the fourteenth century, in unwarmed rooms, lit only by unglazed windows, to have been lectures mainly "expository"; though partly, if you will, designed to "stimulate interest" as well as to convey information. They were, at any rate, public lectures open to the University, and the scholars attending them habitually (one understands) either assiduously took notes or wrote up digests afterwards.

This was before the foundation of colleges, and the gradual growth of that collegiate tutorial system which has been the peculiar development and glory of Oxford and Cambridge among European Universities, and possibly therefore by successive Commissions the main object of attack. It survives and, I hope, always will survive, because based on the most excellent way of all instruction —that of "reading with a man," as the saying went. Of some experience—in youth as a disciple, in age as a teacher—I will testify that the best I have ever received, and feel to have given, has been in private talk over difficulties and enthusiasms, when, across the hearth, one advised and the other questioned, responding. *Iron sharpeneth iron. So a man sharpeneth the counten-*

ance of his friend. Nor do I forget "reading-parties" in moorland farm-houses or by the sea —the rigorous morning bathe followed by Plato or Thucydides.

> And sometimes I remember days of old
> When fellowship seem'd not so far to seek,
>   And all the world and I seem'd much less cold,
>   And at the rainbow's foot lay surely gold,
> And hope was strong, and life itself not weak.

VIII

But now, and increasingly, with the pressure of numbers upon our Universities, these opportunities of quiet tutorial talk grow rarer; and, concurrently, with a marriage fellowship, the old-time hospitable don cycles or motors home to domestic bliss. And so we come to the "expository" or "class" lecture, which I have now, if I can, to defend.

Again I shall begin with an admission. There are too many of them—that is to say, not too many *given*, but far too many *attended*. In my experience it has always been so with members of the Women's Colleges attached to this University; indeed, of women candidates for our

English Tripos at Cambridge I can scarcely remember one in these fourteen years who did not
frequent too many lectures, to the obstruction
of much time that should have been spent in
reading or the less pleasant disciplines of thinking
and learning to write. And now, with the intro-
duction of the "Faculty System," with an in-
clusive fee and a multiplication of lectures, with
hours so thoughtfully arranged that any poor
fellow inclined to get the most for his money
may contrive to sit at the feet, maybe, of some
twenty of us a week—which is merely to invite
mental dyspepsia and lethargy—I find that even
our young men incline to the bad habit. In short,
over-indulgence in being lectured-to is a prim-
rose path to intellectual sloth, the more fatally
deceitful because it looks virtuous.

Thus far, giving its proper precedence to youth,
I have been urging in the main that you attend
too many lectures for a youthful soul's health.
I turn now to put in a plea for the instructors
of youth up here—that they are compelled to
give too many lectures, and generally, apart from
lecturing, to scatter themselves about a great deal
too much, to the dissipation of energy that
might be far more useful in the end were it

allowed more quiet hours in which to concentrate upon thought and reading.

I shall try to speak dispassionately on this point, as I may claim to speak disinterestedly, since the statute prescribing the duties of my own Chair expressly includes that of delivering lectures—

> And otherwise to promote, so far as may be in his power, the study in the University of the subject of English Literature.

For the first, I may urge that, until given respite by a generous University from this desk, and for an infirmity of the eyes now promised to be curable, though not yet cured, I have tried to perform the duty: for the second, that I have been faithful to it. At any rate, *I* cannot complain.

But I speak of quite other men—men who, for their learning only, have been advanced, often in purblindness of the why or how, to be professors in our great Universities; men intent on minute scholarship or research—inexpert in lecturing, careless even of acquiring the art—haters of crowds, of the market-place, not despisers necessarily, but withdrawn rather by instinct to fulfil their best in Room *Theta* here, or in the

circle of their own reading-lamps, impelled only
by the passion (strange to so many practitional
men on this sublunary planet) to learn and to go
on learning. You get the true note of such lives
in Browning's "A Grammarian's Funeral"—

Carry this man's corpse up to the hill-summit :
    He's for the morning ! . . .
This man decided not to live but know—
    Bury this man there !
Here—here's the place, where meteors shoot, clouds
    storm,
    Lightnings are loosened,
Stars come and go ! let joy break with the storm,
    Peace let the dew send !
Lofty designs must close in like effects :
    Loftily lying
Leave him—still loftier than the world suspects,
    Living and dying.

And such men are priceless, though themselves
caring little that their lamps—

    At midnight hour
Be seen on some high lonely tower.

To make particular application—if with reverence I may—it will not be contended of the two
greatest Professors of Latin in the generation
before ours—J. E. B. Mayor here, or Robinson
Ellis at Oxford—that either was an attractive, or

even an articulate, lecturer.   Of Mayor it is told
yet that his initial audience would consist of
three, who, the next week, had shrunk to one.
Of Robinson Ellis at Oxford I recall an inaugural
lecture on a very late and highly erotic Latin
poet, of the worst period; and such a patient,
particular, and intimate exegesis of the human
passions as made the chaperons (there had to
be chaperons for women students in those days)
violently fan themselves.   Yet, while this University possessed a J. E. B. Mayor and Oxford a
Robinson Ellis, while they possess living exemplars to whom the scholarship of Europe instinc-
tively, reverently turns—as, centuries ago, it
turned Bede's candle in Jarrow—it is profanity, I
say, to drag such men down and vulgarise them
in lecture-rooms.   We may try to adorn them.
They adorn *us*, and the last satisfaction of the true
scholar is his solitary turret and his candle shed-
ding its beams like a good deed in a naughty world.

I say that no University can dispense with
such illuminates and illuminants or, save to its peril
in the world's eyes, forgo cherishing and protecting
them; for they are few, and most venerable.   Nay,
I go farther and assert the fashion of considering
our Universities as founded solely for the educa-

tion and moral government of youth to be
exorbitant, as it certainly lacks warrant of history.
By "seats of learning," believe me, was never
meant, exclusively, a congregation of benches on
which young men sat to learn, any more than the old
term "the Bishop's Stool" for a cathedral connoted
three wooden legs.   Let me refer you back for
a moment to Sidgwick's description of his first
lecture in a German University.   His indictment
lay against the listeners' waste of time over note-
taking which they might have spent more usefully
on reading the words in a printed book.   But
might he not—the lecturer having been a person of
eminence and renown—have considered also the
waste of *that man's* time with his yellow manuscript?

To descend from these solitary and rarefied
heights of difficult breathing—

> What pleasure lives in height (the shepherd sang),
> In height and cold, the splendour of the hills?

—and to put in a plea for more accessible, more
companionable, if less learned, instructors—

You overtax them daily and nightly throughout
term—you really do.   Putting lectures and classes
aside, we are sued for extramural discourses, for
talks to literary or scientific societies, University
and College clubs;   for contributions to this or

that magazine; to read and give advice upon (say) such outputs of original verse as would astonish you even more by their mass than by their originality; and if unguarded encouragement should accompany the advice, to find them a publisher, even to write a "Foreword" (before those two terrible Anglo-Saxon syllables take shape one foresees them, with foreknowledge absolute, and winces), with the always pleasant business of being consulted by a man about his work, and the always painful expectation of the "testimonial" to be written later. Yes, and there is a class of man who seems to require a rare and refreshing testimonial at intervals of six months.

Now, within my experience of Cambridge, this tax upon your privileged instructors has grown and grown, out of all proportion to its convenience, use, or profit; and in addition to these unofficial demands, there has been laid on us the burden of "supervising" candidates for the novel and (to my thinking) superfluous degree of Ph.D.—a concession by Oxford and Cambridge to a commercial value of titles in the United States— and a degree for which, in my experience, as yet no single American researcher in English has ever qualified himself, while, our initial conception of "research" being entirely more stringent, not one pupil from these Islands or our King's dominions has ever missed the mark. It is accurately 100 against 100 in my own supervisory work of English here; and while the report of a single experience may not for a while, in its small way, encourage international relations, it may *help* towards an ultimate understanding of what two great nations are agreed upon as a standard of English research.

But to resume—it is evident to me that, since the War, one does know the old conversation of a Cambridge Combination Room—no longer in any degree comparable with that of the old days when we met and had leisure to talk kindly over our undergraduates for their benefit; and the kindliness of a college system towards its sometimes peccant undergraduates cannot be overestimated. [I speak of some acquaintance with two Universities.] From the High Table we rush now to many and multifarious engagements. It tires us; it dissipates—though it be but by that familiarity which breeds contempt—our true authority, our real use amongst you. I recall the old flippant remark of an undergraduate to his tutor, that he for his part didn't think much of a college fellow's life, and the quiet retort,

"Sir, it has at least this excuse for itself. Of all vocations it is the most easily avoided."

So I am not complaining quite selfishly of all this fuss and ferment and harrying of old quiet friends. But I will put it thus—for *your* sakes. Do you really think all this fuss of lectures, audiences, and worrying of older men, to be *good for you*? Had you not better be employed—if I may recur upon my ideal University of Youth—in worrying out things for yourselves? Let us take your Union Society, for example. In former days it was a *palæstra*—an arena in which young men met their match, wrestled, learned their trade by practice, the better man coming, if gradually, by practice to fit himself for Parliament. Nowadays what increasingly happens? A President's term of office is praised for the number of star politicians he can, by hook or crook, persuade to come down for a gladiatorial show; and after these gladiators have played their part, condescendingly, in a show combat, the audience fades away. Is that not a fair description? But is it, for use, a preparation comparable with the old intellectual gymnastic which here, in Cambridge, bred and trained statesmen?

Great practitioners you may invite to Cambridge for *examples*—as you may go over to Newmarket to learn how a perfectly trained horse can run, and be the better for that knowledge. But if you go there not knowing one end of a horse from another, you are simply in the position of one who comes up to this place, ignoring its breed, its trained intellectual movement—all that ancestrally a great University means; satisfied with gladiators cheaply hired by flattery.

IX

I shall be asked, of course—I feel the silent question arising—"Why, then,—holding that lectures are too many—announce on your English Tripos list so many lectures on so many subjects?"

But I answer that question easily. Our English Tripos is designed, not to detect what you *don't* know—a feat perhaps as easy as it were certainly unprofitable—but to discover what you *do*. The examination paper gives you some twenty questions or more, of which you are almost forbidden to answer more than five. If you will bear this in mind, as also that any single examiner would probably shirk answering every question set, to blush for the sum of his attempts, you may convince yourselves, Gentlemen, that our English school here is, even in a secondary sense, one of the "Humaner Letters."

But let us go, for the purpose of adjusting our English Tripos to it, a little deeper into the idea of a University—the "thing it was meant to be."

In the first place, then, the function of a University is by no means merely to impart knowledge to you. Among other purposes, perhaps for the most vital of any, you are here to learn to *think* for yourselves; to have your minds to a certain extent liberated after the stricter and more disciplinary instruction of school. Your college gown in fact is a *toga virilis*, and you have come to the age to wear it. This liberation gives, of course, no license to sudden anarchy of mind or unbridled egoism in conduct; the Statutes, so far as they can, release you gradually and gently. You are undergraduates, still *in statu pupillari* though with the dignity already of being a University man—which means literally and historically "one of us." In due course, let us hope, you will all advance through the degree of Bachelor to a Mastership of Arts. You may even —if you value it—proceed to a Doctorate in some branch of learning. But a Mastership of Arts implies, or should imply, that you have taken such advantage of three or four years here that you have so far acquired—by help of your dons, and by rubbing your intelligence in a large and jostling concourse of youth—a chastened and corrected liberty of your own thought, with a responsibility for it which sends you out with a grip of affairs and a persuasive mastery over your own and other men's minds, whether your vocation be the Court, the Bar, or Teaching, or the modest service of a Country Parish; in all— to quote the words of the Catechism so often misunderstood—"to learn and labour truly to get mine own living, and to do my duty in that state of life into which it shall please God to call me." Service, in other words; service in whatever capacity, with a mastery learnt here, but a mastery of service. Our English moralists have never, any more than the Greeks, been able to divorce ethics from politics, or separate a citizen from his duty to the State.

Now much and intricate learning is, of course, a service to the State. It increases knowledge, and may increase wisdom. But it does not *necessarily* increase wisdom; it is seldom achieved in the course of an undergraduate career; and if accumulated without digestion, may fatally clog the process of thinking for yourself. Among many learned men I have known and reverenced, some have been the least *civilised* of the species.

After all, the four Platonic cardinal virtues—the old quadrilateral—remain respectable in our commonwealth: Justice, Wisdom, Manliness, and *Sophrosynè*—an almost untranslatable word which I shall presently try to explain. "Justice" is, in the end, an adjustment; man's fitting himself and his conduct to the scheme of things, to harmonise them in government and in social relations. "Wisdom" is that "part" of him which instructs him to do this rationally; curbing that which is headstrong or excessive in the third virtue "Manliness," while training that virtue, as discipline trains a brave fighter to be a soldier. The success of our Universities here, the law-abiding spirit of sport, the value of "team-work" practised on river, on cricket and football fields, leapt to the eye in August 1914, when our sons sprang to arms to prove themselves soldiers and the officers of soldiery, with a quickness so nearly miraculous that even believers caught their breath.

But the fourth, the "royal" virtue of "Sophro-synè" is (as I have said) an idea almost untrans-latable into any word—even into its own Greek name. Socrates—as anyone would expect—had a try at defining it, but gave it up. It was not "temperance" (even in the right sense of "temper-ance"). Temperance would not cover it, though temperance entered into the idea. Nor "modesty," save by exclusion, inhibiting self-assertion, self-consciousness, rash arrogance. It is more than "tranquillity," though by nature and character "tranquil," since (to use a phrase of Marcus Aurelius) "it makes for itself no solitudes, no hermitages, no retiring place but the man's own soul," and is most evidently useful in practical affairs, public affairs, crises, hours of peril; as a good ship's-captain, reliant on his seamanship, is calmest in a gale, or a good statesman amid violent disturbances. It is disinterested; it despises low joys, low gains.

Disdains whatever Cornbury disdains.

On this side it stands unalterably opposed, as the spirit of Athens was opposed, proudly against the commercial, oligarchical spirit of Corinth where (as the Athenians held) men had given over the command of their souls, with cold-blooded calculation, to money and the sensual gratifications which money can buy. This untranslatable word, *sophrosynè*, says Mr A. E. Taylor—possibly the best understander of Plato in our day, and of what Plato was driving at—

> has been variously rendered in English by "temperance," "continence," "self-control," equivalents which are all objectionable from the implication of painful self-constraint which they carry with them.

Yes, it comes of no constraint; but rather of liberty, the genial use of liberty. Attempting the impossible, I might try to define it to you as "assured mental grace," decorating and distinguishing its happy possessor as, in the old common phrase, "a scholar and a gentleman," quietly conscious of his limits, quietly aware that it takes all sorts to make a world, while as quietly sure that, of his intellectual breeding, he can enter any company of the wise and listen to what the wise may have to tell him. But he goes home and refers the sayings of the wisest to his own inward monitor. For he has a mind of his own, suppled, annealed, tempered by a high and (so far as the gods have endowed him) *a celestial common-sense*; he knows, with the Son of Siraeh, that "a man's mind is sometime wont to tell him more than seven watchmen that sit above in a high tower," and that therefore with his gifts, however modestly he may rate them, he has the responsibility of thinking for himself. "So," says Pascal—one of the noblest exemplars of this "royal science"—"in dealing with men your words will be the fewer but the more effective."

I make no apology for dwelling at length on this virtue of *Sophrosynè*, because, to begin with, its meaning eludes terse definition (as do the meanings of most things priceless in life, since, being priceless, they cannot be appraised); and secondly, because it is the very crown of a University education.

Such a virtue is perhaps better conveyed to the mind by instances than by any attempted definition. In my first lecture at Cambridge, some fourteen years ago, I quoted Lucian's description of his friend Demonax:

His way was like other people's: he mounted no high horse: he was just a man and a citizen. He indulged in no Socratic irony. But his discourse was full of Attic grace: those who heard it went away neither disgusted by servility nor repelled by ill-tempered conceits, but on the contrary lifted out of themselves by charity, and encouraged to more orderly, contented, useful lives,

and I went on to say that Demonax, thus affectionately presented to us out of a friend's memory, must have been at once a scholar and a gentleman —in short, just of the type that our Universities should aim to turn out and take pride in as justified of their children.

So far so good, maybe. But it is rather on the business of setting their feet on the way of this intellectual grace than of completing it within a year or two's course that a University must rest its hopes. Youth, learning to use liberty, is naturally, rightly, a time of ferment, and subsidence from ferment is the secret of all good wine, often the more valuable for being slowly mellowed in a youth of "comet year." Given the aptitude to learn, you must allow age (I plead) its share in the ripening process. Or let me put it that if, at twenty-three or so, a youth already answers the aspiration once addressed by Sir John Denham to the River Thames—

O, could I flow with thee, and make thy stream
My great example, as it is my theme!
Though deep, yet clear; though gentle, not too dull;
Strong without rage; without o'erflowing full,

he might perchance, by intensive culture, satisfy a tutor's idea of *Sophrosynè*; but quite as likely the rest of the world would pronounce him a first-class prig.

Well, I have only to say here that, if my illustration be inadequate or do injustice to youth, the great Plato himself, in the *Charmides* and *Theœtetus*, introduces two young Greeks as admirable specimens of *Sophrosynè*, only to interrogate them on that virtue and leave the undefinable undefined.

X

Still on this point I shall here, with your leave, insist as definite that, through the heap of accumulated knowledge and past piles of books, the true business of a University is to train liberty into responsibility, to teach a young man to think for himself, yet so as he remembers he is a citizen, and of no mean city. And so after this digression—which is really no digression—let us hark back to practice.

It should be the business, then, of any wise tutor or supervisor to direct your reading and your choice (preferably economical) of lectures.

And—on the evidence of the class-lists I may
settle it now without any fear of our school
being called a "soft option"—the range of our
literature being so vast, he will be the wiser if
he counsel you, after discussing it, to concentrate
on this or that point of your own propensities
and follow in earnest the lines that ray out from
them. Nor is it indispensable that the student
be sent to lecturers of repute, save to learn
how they handle their themes. In the third
century, for example, the great Plotinus chose
—as Origen chose likewise—and attended for ten
years, out of many teachers more famous in their
time, one Ammonius Saccus, called "the Porter,"
a teacher of mean estate, who committed nothing
to writing. Plotinus, in his own words, chose
him because "This is the man I was looking for";
and Plotinus himself, when he had made his fame
in Rome, for long, until between fifty and sixty
years of age, refused to commit his lectures to writing. He believed in the oral way of communicat-
ing truth. We are told by Porphyry, his disciple,
that he would allow his auditors to break the
thread of his discourse by asking questions, was
shy and nervous, almost too patient of any honest
objector who propounded a difficulty.

XI

This (you see) brings me back, in dealing with "class" lectures, to the matter of question and interruption: and on this point Plutarch—himself a practised lecturer—has, I think, said the last word. After telling us, as I have quoted him, that a youth is at all times to find silence a credit to him, and especially at a lecture, he proceeds—

That is, where he can listen to another without becoming excited and vocal; where, even if what is said be little to his liking, he waits for the speaker to finish; when at the close of a paragraph he does not come instantly to the attack but (to quote Æschines) "waits and sees," in case the lecturer may supplement, or adjust or qualify his argument. To take instant objection, when both parties will be talking at once, is unseemly. They, on the other hand, who have learnt to listen with a discreet self-control will receive an argument and make it their own at its worth, while in a better position to expose one that is false or flimsy, thereby showing themselves to be lovers of truth and not headstrong persons, argumentative, prone to a quarrel. Wherefore it is not a bad remark of some that there is more need (I am still quoting Plutarch) to expel the wind of vanity from the young than the air from a wine-skin if you wish to decant a wine of sound vintage. A skin previously distended will hardly do it justice.

Plato's own answer (if you remember) to a pert interruption was, "Am I, perhaps, so bad?" And I recall the answer given in my own time by a scholar of European renown to a confident youth—"Ah, yes, you have the advantage of me, sir! You have looked the word up in *Liddell and Scott*, that admirable lexicon."

Before a listener interrupts midway in a "class" lecture he should bethink himself that it hinders not only the man at the desk, but mayhap the whole auditory, who do not share his immediate difficulty, but are impatient to hear on. In fact, he may too easily find himself, like the proverbial dog in the tennis-court, the enemy of everyone.

It seems to me, then, that in "class" lectures, as in public lectures, all interruptions should be ruled out; that the lecturer should confine his words within fifty minutes or even less; and that afterwards, in a retiring-room, he should listen to any listener's difficulty, or—if he be tired and the difficulty serious—appoint a time to discuss it privately in his college rooms.

XII

You see, gentlemen, that I am always harking back upon the Platonic method of dialectic, and that is just because I have experimentally proved it, to believe in it, more than in any other. The Dialogues of Plato give the obstetric Socrates more than his share in the parturition of Platonic thought, and Adeimantus' share in those incomparable writings is too closely confined to "Quite so" or "I fail to follow." But Socrates was Socrates, and in the art of disputation can be granted all his pre-eminence.

I yet claim that for smaller teachers his way— or Plato's way—was the best ever invented for opening the mind; for adapting the experience of us elders to questions by our juniors; for agreement that it takes both young and old to conspire for a decent world. Good books have improved it, but so have lecturers whose names are now but a repute—some eminent, but many inferior, who yet by their earnestness had the gift to attract, to compel audiences in their day.